DUNSOP 1
Bowland Forest

With illustrations by
SHEILA CARTER
and
JANNA JÄRVINEN

JOHN DIXON

Dunsop Bridge
Bowland Forest

By
John Dixon

With illustrations by
Sheila Carter and Janna Järvinen

Published by Aussteiger Publications,
21 Lowergate, Clitheroe BB7 1AD

Typeset by
Rebecca Carter and David Bunyan

Printed by
Lamberts Print & Design, Station Road, Settle,
North Yorkshire BD24 9AA

First Edition 2003

ISBN 1 872764 08 8

To the memory of Mr Chris Spence
of Burholme

Contents

EXCURDIUM

THIS IS MY first book in ten years, and it is good to be back on 'home' ground.

In those years I gained and lost in love, tried farming on a small island in the Libian Sea, opened a B&B in Haworth, worked as an electrical engineer at Rolls Royce, bought a tiny cottage in Clitheroe and was hospitalized with a mental condition twice! Some decade.

My kids are adults now; Wayne works with disadvantaged young people in London and has become a poet, Maxine is a hair stylist and soon off to the USA – God help Uncle Sam.

I thought of moving to another planet, but Puddleducks Phillip twisted my arm to write this book – I shall never forgive him.

Iain Hogg, the blacksmith at Black Boar Forge, dragged me over hill and dale, fed me mints that made my teeth fall out and forged me a Viking Ship gate to go with my boots.

Sheila Carter took control of my 'wayword' writing and is enlightening me to the ways of green things that grow and the creatures of the Good Earth – a hard taskmistress.

Mum and Dad gave me their old computer, so I am now forced into the Modern Age – goodbye old plink-plonk typewriter friend.

Colin next door puts up with my CD player pumping out Johnny Cash, Chet Atkins, Mark Knoffler, Dolly Parton and Charlie Feathers at all hours of the day and night.

I no longer drink hard liquor, thanks to David Hazell, but still smoke excise-free Dutch tabac, my only vice – fibber.

Any errors in this book are the fault of those mentioned above, not mine. I'm off to live in a yurt, by the rivers of Babylon. See you all soon in Ribchester – look out Nora here I come.

Look after yourselves and be kind.

John.

DUNSOP BRIDGE

DUNSOP IS FIRST recorded in a land grant by King Athelstan to the church of St. Peter in the city of York, when he appointed Wulfstan archbishop there, of land called Amounderness, namely from the sea up the Cocker to its source, thence directly to a spring called Dunsop and descending that stream to the Hodder and then into the Ribble and so on by the mid-stream to the sea. Given at Nottingham, 7th June, 930.

The exact Centre of Great Britain, complete with its 401 principal offshore islands, has been determined by the Ordnance Survey to be at National Grid reference SD63770 56550. This is above the Brennand Valley on Brown Syke Moss, 600m west of the Whitendale Hanging Stones. The nearest village is Dunsop Bridge.

The land is a water-catchment area for United Utilities and walkers are permitted except during the grouse season.

To commemorate the classification British Telecom chose Dunsop Bridge as the location for their 100,000th payphone. The phone box was unveiled by the Arctic explorer Sir Ranulph Fiennes at an official ceremony held on June 29th, 1992.

The phone box has an etched-glass design, showing key place-names around Great Britain. Wooden posts represent the four main points of the compass and inside the kiosk is a plaque giving the precise co-ordinates for the Centre if the Kingdom.

Dunsop Bridge, with safe car-parking and good clean toilets, makes for a great place for a family day out. You may wish only to sit by the riverside and feed the ducks, but I hope that my little book will encourage you to venture further and gain a true feel of this lovely section of the Hodder Valley.

BOLLAND FOREST

BEFORE THE NORMAN Conquest Bolland Forest was a true forest area being well timbered up to 1650ft. ASL, holly, hazel, oak and ash flourished. Alder, as today, dominated the edges of the water meadows.

Recent changes in land use have led to new farming innovations. A policy of re-establishing wooded areas and hedgerows has begun. In time, the results of these efforts will prove to be spectacular – a great step forward in sustaining the rural environment.

Tourism must complement this change and the farming community must be involved on a real basis – tourism can be a great income generator.

Local families must be helped to remain and work in the area and their needs must have priority over wealthy incomers. Without these Folk and their good labour the Forest of Bowland will become nothing more than a playground for rich city people.

The near landscape is valuable and lovable because of its nearness; it is where children are reared and what they take away in their minds to their long future.

PUDDLEDUCKS

COUNTRY STORE, POST OFFICE AND TEA ROOM

In January 2000 Philip and Janette Woodhead took over and renovated the Village Shop, Puddleducks, selling ice creams, groceries, local produce and a wide range of gifts at very reasonable prices.

Puddlesducks Tearooms was opened for business that Easter. With its flag floor and pine furniture, it is the ideal place to head for at the start or end of your walk.

Philip – no stranger to catering has attracted a loyal clientele who return for his 'bungo' soup (into which everything is bunged), hot meals – all prepared and made by himself and his selection of hot puddings and homemade cakes.

Lunches served 12pm–2pm

Puddleducks tearoom is open 6 days a week 9:30am–4:30pm
Closed Mondays

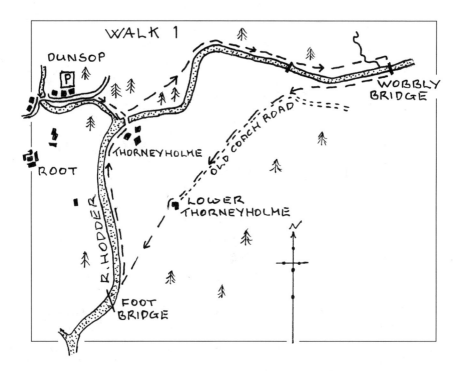

WALK 1

LOCAL MYTH AND LEGEND

2 miles easy walking along the riverside and through meadows.

Asleep for most of the day the old man of Bollard dreams of feasting on a tasty sugar loaf. In the dead of the night the old man awakens and makes his way quietly along the moonlit valley to bite into his favorite delight. Rarely does he get more than one small bite of the confection as the place where sweet cake stands is guarded by a nasty black boggart. The boggart is wise to the old man's fancy and taunts him out of his wits, laughing hideously as the poor old fellow flees in terror back to his bed below Totridge. Local greedy beggars who, having outwitted the boggart, have tried to feast on the loaf have received a suspended sentence for their efforts.

"What on earth is he on about?' you may ask. Follow me and all will become clear.

DUNSOP BRIDGE TO WOBBLY BRIDGE

On leaving the car park turn left and walk along the road a short way to enter the tree-lined driveway of Thorneyholme on the right, as the road bends to the left.

The Giant Redwoods.

Let us stop for a moment and take in this avenue of Giant Redwoods. This species, the Wellingtonia (sequoiadendron giganteum), was found growing in the California Mountains in 1852 and introduced to England in 1853. In California trunks 25 metres in girth have been measured being over 3,000 years old, while in

Britain the trees have grown to 8 metres in girth over 120 years. These trees will grow to a height of 38 metres. The thick, deeply furrowed bark appears rough and hard yet it is surprisingly soft and spongy to the touch. This is because it does not contain any resin making it also fire-resistant. The tree was named in memory of the Duke of Wellington who died at the time of the discovery.

The trees are said to hold the spirits of long dead Native American Indian's and it is unlucky to cut one down or do it harm.

I shall not rest quiet within this tree
I shall not be there, I shall rise and pass
Bury my heart in Wounded Knee

Walk along the drive and as you approach the bridge leave the drive to pass through a kissing gate on the left. Cross the field and go over a footbridge into the trees. Follow the river up, passing the aqueduct, within 20 paces of a footbridge.

Looking to the north the eye picks out a curiously shaped limestone reef knoll. This is the Knot or Sugar Loaf. The south face of the hill has been quarried and a kiln built below the quarry floor.

Essentially the kiln is a large stone built bowl with a grate at the base for drawing out lime and ashes. Alternating layers of broken limestone and fuel were stacked in the kiln then fired. The lime was used to improve sour land on the uplands, and in building work for mortar, plaster and limewash. Most farmers had their own kiln and would run the kiln for weeks at a time.

In former times a gibbet stood upon Sugar Loaf displaying the chained corpse of some poor soul reduced to felony. This was intended as a warning and deterrent to others. The gibbet chains were found in a nearby hedgerow sometime ago.

Walk onto the footbridge.

Here the boundary stream of Rough Syke, having gurgled down from the Hidden Valley of Echoes, meets the Hodder. The cut of the syke from here to the deserted Moor End above the valley road is the

The Sugar Loaf

haunt of a black boggart, often sighted on the parapet of the road bridge.

A boggart is a fearful creature, a local hobgoblin that haunts a gloomy spot or scene of violence. No local will wander hereabouts after darkness has descended.

Recently the boggart was spotted early one morning by Water Authority workmen who were startled by what they thought to be an enormous feline creature. The incident was reported in the Clitheroe newspaper. So give a thought to those unquiet spirits that cannot reach that realm of pure White Light that upon death leads to the beyond.

Kingfisher

Cross the bridge and stile and walk on to the suspension bridge.

The bridge looks fearsome and wobbles a little, but is very safe. It is one of two that cross the Hodder and provide good spots for observing river life.

Trout, even salmon, in the deep pools of the Hodder may sometimes be seen leaping clear of the water. Sea trout are running in June, and brown trout are very common. Salmon return from Greenland to spawn in December. Bullheads, stone louch and minnows are numerous.

The heron stalks its prey in the shallows of the river – as still as a grey wizened post, till it strikes. Look out also for the little kingfisher with its large head, dagger-like beak, and electric turquoise plumage.

Heron

Leave the suspension bridge and a riverside path on the right leads us to pass through the two gates. Then walk up to the left to pass through a gateway onto the trackway.

We are now standing on the old coach road linking Thorneyholme with the village of Newton.

The old road leads us down into the farmyard at Lower Thorneyholme via field gates. Turn left at corner of barn and walk on, through gateway to cross the rough land of Star Bar to reach the riverbank.

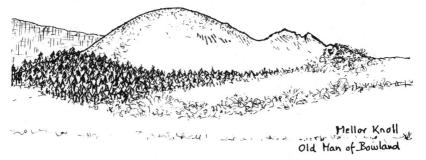

Mellor Knoll
Old Man of Bowland

THE OLD MAN OF BOLLAND

The skyline before us is dominated by the broad back of Totridge Fell, below which is the bare hill of Mellor Knoll – locally referred to as the 'Old Man of Bolland."

The hill has the appearance of a rotund gentleman sleeping the afternoon away after a lunchtime session in the Whitewell. During the summer months the leafy foliage gives the Old Man a fine crop of curly hair. We shall leave him peacefully dreaming, lulled by the waters' song and wander back upriver to the Café at Dunsop.

Cross over the stile by the tree on your right and walk up the riverside to the bridge at Thorneyholme and back to Dunsop.

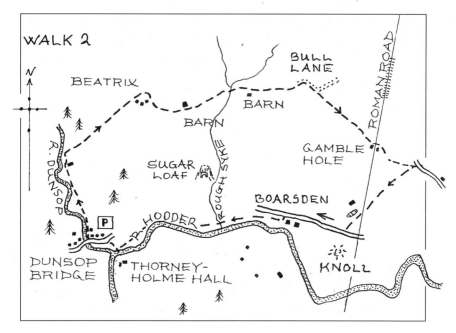

WALK 2

THE HIDDEN VALLEY

5 miles easy walking along undulating hillside pastures and river-side meadows. Allow 3 hours for this delightful ramble.

Tucked away below Burn Fell and Beatrix there is a hidden valley known only to the few. It has no name on any map, but locals refer to it as the Valley of Echoes. Shout and your voice comes back from the age-old farmsteads below the wild fell side. Here, over a thousand years ago, Norse Vikings settled to tame the wilderness, turning swords into ploughshares and putting roving behind them. The landscape that we wander through today is the culmination of their efforts. Though long gone an association survives in river, fell and farm names. So without further ado let us be on our way.

DUNSOP TO BEATRIX

Walk along the lane by the side of 'puddleducks', passing the children's activity area, and Jenny Barn to the rear of Holme Head cottages. Pass through the gateway and walk on a short way to go over a stile on the right where wooden steps take you up to the meadow. When crossing the

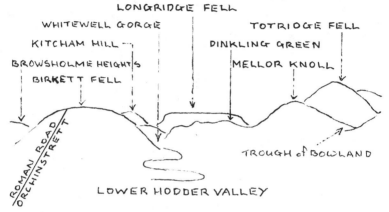

meadow stop when Beatrix comes into view and take in the prospect down the Hodder Valley – one of the most beautiful and gratifying that I know. The path now follows the overhead power lines to the farm lane at Beatrix.

Beatrix takes its name from a Viking who first settled here in the 10th century – Bothvar was one of many Hiberno-Norse colonists who came over

BEATRIX

from the Norwegian kingdom of Dublin to farm the marginal lands on the edges of established Anglo-British settlements. Those with the surname of Battersby may claim descent from this wild sea-rover turned farmer.

Today only two homesteads nestle between two fell side streams where once stood a hamlet of six holdings and an Inn. Beatrix had been an important stock-rearing centre since the early 13th century, and markets were held here in the 17th and 18th centuries. Three other holdings stood on the edge of the settlement. One of these has grown from a simple blacksmith's forge into the modern village of Dunsop Bridge. The other two, Holme Head and Wood End, have changed little from their original size. Remains of the old village are few, but the careful eye will pick out old door heads and window mullions built into the fabric of the surrounding farm walls.

On a recent visit to the Forest of Bowland Her Majesty the Queen paid a visit to Beatrix to admire the view down the Hodder Valley, which her great grandmother, Queen Victoria, had spoken of as being a 'Little Switzerland.' Queen Elizabeth said that the verdant valley

landscape well deserved the appellation and could consider herself living in such a pleasing setting.

BEATRIX TO GAMBLE HOLE

The lane leads up to the higher farmyard to pass through the left-hand field gate and follow the cart track around to Back o' t' Hill Barn.

Now we stand above and look upon the 'Hidden Valley of Echoes.' Best responses to be had beyond Rough Syke Barn.

This is curlew and oyster-catcher country, both ground nesting birds. In spring the curlew will skulk away from the nest, it will fly around, yelping above you. The parti-coloured oystercatcher stands out clearly in the meadow grass. Notice its long red bill. Meadow pipets or skylark may startle you as they flutter from their nests in the tufts of course vegetation.

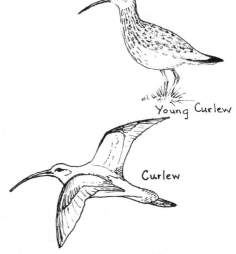

Young Curlew

Curlew

The old out barn here belongs to a former farming tradition. It would have held a stock of hay and had tying-up for about twelve young cattle, which remained here the winter through, gradually consuming the hay and being released daily to drink from the water trough.

This barn along with many others in the district is now redundant and it would be a great loss to see it fall into a state of dereliction as is the case with Rough Syke Barn standing across the valley. Rough Syke was a good example of an early 18th century barn – a solid oak truss–framed roof, good local stonework displaying a segmental arched main doorway. Sadly the time of writing, Winter 2003, the west gable wall is in a state of collapse – so keep away. Restoration of these barns could provide housing for local people or camping barns for use by visitors to the area.

Walk down the field to go over stile by field-gate and on to cross stream and stile.

Notice the eight huge stone slabs bridging the beck, and another six slabs spanning the higher beck.

A good track takes us up, passing Rough Syke Barn, to go over a stile by field-gate.

Stop and take in the vista from here – magnificent.

Walk up to enter Bull Lane via stile by gate. Walk on, turn the corner and on down to a small wall-gate at next corner.

Bull Lane, a wide thorn – lined enclosed track way, is reminiscent of the old mid-Pennine drove roads. Older inhabitants of the valley tell of it being part of an old road that once ran from the village of Beatrix to Wood House above Slaidburn. Today it is a haven for a wide variety of plant life. In early spring, cow parsley and sweet cicely give a frothy white edging to the track. The latter was once used to flavor stews – crush a leaf and you will smell aniseed.

Pass through the gate and walk down the field of limestone 'shake holes' to Gamble Hole farm gate.

GAMBLE HOLE

No, the name does not refer to the huge hollow before us. That hole was once a lime quarry complex. The mouth of the kiln is   buried in the face opposite – your eye will just pick out three or four stones from the access arch above a hole.

Gamble Hole

The shake holes in the fields were formed by soil and clay being absorbed by fissures in the underlying limestone, creating a grassy funnel. Some of these have been mined for silver and lead.

The old name of Gamble Hole was 'Gamellearges,' meaning 'Gamel's cattle pasture.' Gamel was another Viking settler who once farmed land between Brung Hill and Lamb Hill above Slaidburn an area traversed by a Roman military road between the cavalry forts of Ribchester and Burrow in Lonsdale. The line of the road passes through the farmyard below

GAMBLE HOLE TO DUNSOP BRIDGE

Pass through the small side gate and walk down to the cattle-grid. Take the cart track to your right and follow the line of trees to go over a corner wall-stile hidden behind the last tree. Walk down the field to pass through a gate at far left-hand corner, and immediately over wall-stile on right. Walk directly on, through corner squeeze-stile and on down by line of trees to cross some rough ground to find a fence-stile in the hedgerow below Heaning trout farm. Cross the driveway and walk directly on by line of fence to go over stile by gate.

We are now again standing on the line of the Roman road.

Walk directly on to go over field-stile onto the road.

The wooded limestone outcrop opposite is the Knoll, from which Knowlmere takes its name. The face we see has been quarried for building stone.

Turn right and walk down the road to Boarsden farm. Just beyond the farm entry roads you will find a footpath sign. Pass through the gate and walk between buildings to go through Dixon's garden gate on your right. Here a green track leads us down to the riverside.

What a splendid view of the gateway to the Trough of Bowland!

Walk on, passing the suspension bridge, to go over stile and Rough Syke Footbridge. Cross the field and on by the river, passing the aqueduct (FWB 1925,) to enter small riverside copse then cross footbridge into field. Cross the field directly to Thorneyholme drive, via iron kissing-gate. Walk down the Redwood drive to the café and car park at Dunsop.

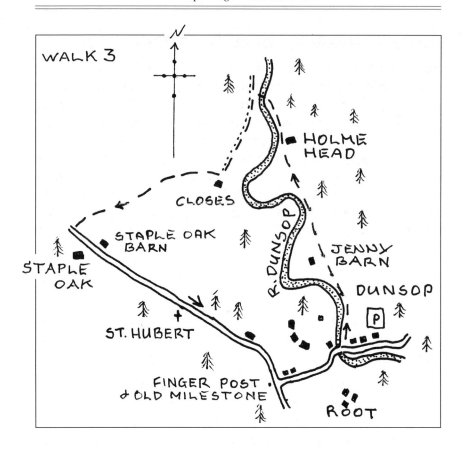

WALK 3

BOWLAND FOREST CHAPEL

A short easy walk of 2 miles, allow 1 1/2 hours.

Today we gain views up the forested Dunsop Valley and visit a remote chapel in the Trough of Bowland. There is a little road walking so walk facing the oncoming traffic and keep an eye on the children.

DUNSOP BRIDGE TO ST. HUBERT'S

Look out for the dipper bobbing from stone to stone as we walk by the river. It has a white bib and chocolate-brown plumage. Rabbits will be busy in the woods and thrushes and blackbirds will be scuffling under the hedgerows at a springtime visit.

Walk along the lane by the side of the Post Office, passing the children's activity area and Jenny Barn to the rear of Holme Head cottages.

dipper

The winner of the 1861 Derby, Kettledrum, was stabled here at Holme Head and trained in the fields nearby.

Pass through the gate and walk on to go over a footbridge.

Looking up the pined-lined valley we could easily be in the wild Highlands of Scotland – in fact, you can walk from here on footpaths all the way to Scotland without passing through any towns.

This is hawk country. Look out for the hen harrier (logo of the Forest of Bowland,) kestrel, buzzard, merlin and, if you are very lucky, the peregrine falcon.

In the early hours of the morning deer come out of the woodland to drink by the waters edge. Sika deer are the most common, being introduced from Asia in the 1860's. Their alarm call is a short, sharp scream, like a whistle. The tiny roe deer can also be seen, the alarm call of the buck is a gruff bark.

Turn left and walk along the road to near the cattle-grid at Closes farm. Walk into the field on your right and walk around the pens to pass through and old iron Towneley estate gate

Red Deer

This is a pheasant breeding area, the poults hand reared. The birds are reared for sport and are a feature of the local economy. The pheasant is a descendant of an ancient Asian jungle fowl. The mating call is a loud, metallic 'korrk-kok.'

Brown hares and rabbits live in this land below the high fells, and so does Reynard the red fox. The red fox

ROE DEER

is very common these days, though rarely seen during the day – early mornings are a good time for sightings. In late January it can be heard barking in the night. This is the dog fox making his presence known to the bitch during the mating season. She, the vixen, can emit a frightening scream.

Walk on by the wall side to the corner above Staple Oak barn.

The Hareden Valley now comes into view, a very wild and remote hunting ground.

Walk on and over to the right to go through gate at the footpath sign onto the Trough road.

The roadway beyond the cattle-grid is the start of that wild mountain pass known as the Trough of Bowland, the side valleys

Pheasant

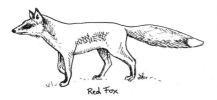

Red Fox

being once the refuge to bands of Outlaws.

Abbot Paslew of Whalley Abbey was brought in chains this way to be tried for Treason at Lancaster Castle and was brought back along the Trough road. To be hung at Little Imps at Whalley.

A cartload of Pendle Witches passed this way in 1612 to suffer their fate at Lancaster – no return trip for them.

COUNTRY TRAMPS

Tramps were once a regular feature of the countryside, but are rarely seen these days.

Before the innovation of the 'cattle-grid' many of the Bowland roads were gated in order to stop cattle and sheep from wandering. Back in the 1950's, I remember seeing the odd tramp sitting by

FOX'S TRACK

such gates waiting for the then infrequent passage of traffic. For a small reward, sixpence, they would give the traveler the time of day, the local weather outlook and open and shut the gate for them. As a boy I thought this a wonderful occupation, one that I should emulate when I grew up.

Bowland's most famous tramp was the eccentric Peregrine Towneley, known as Owd Peregrine. A good tale is recounted as to how he acquired the Bowland Forest Estate for the Towneley family.

This clever, but somewhat erratic old gentleman had always wished to acquire this section of the Hodder Valley, for the scenery is very d e l i g h t f u l . Peregrine, with his innate sense of grim humour, loved a joke, and apparently never cared the least what folk thought of him.

Hearing that the estate was for sale to be auctioned at the Whitewell Inn, he dressed himself in old tattered clothes, and, with a clay pipe in his mouth, wandered up to Whitewell and begged a breakfast at the Inn on the day of the sale. He was given porridge and beans, and when he had finished his repast he strolled into the auction room and enquired what estate was for sale. On being informed that it was the Whitewell Estate, he laughed, and said he might as well make a bid for it himself.

The assembled company was highly amused that an old tramp should presume to bid for the extensive property, and told him that they were awaiting the arrival of the 'big man' of the shire.

"And who is your big man?" enquired the tramp. "Why, Peregrine Towneley, of course," was the reply. "He is coming here today, and his price is sure to be far higher than any other, for everyone knows he is very keen on getting this place."

The tramp said that he would begin the bidding while they were waiting, and thereupon named a ridiculously small sum. There were roars of laughter, and someone by way of carrying on the joke bid a little higher. The tramp went higher still, and then the auctioneer, entering into the fun, knocked down the estate to the old tramp for an absurd amount, under the mistaken belief that he could not possibly pay.

He then asked in derision what name was to be entered in his book as the purchaser of the property, whereupon the unknown traveler

St. Hubert's Church, the Trough Road, Dunsop Bridge

walked up to the desk and laid a small white card bearing the words,
"Mr. Peregrine Towneley,
Towneley Hall, Burnley,"
Before the horrified auctioneer.

Walk down the road to the forest chapel of St. Hubert.

THE FOREST CHAPEL OF ST. HUBERT R. C.

The church was built in 1864 on land donated by the Towneley family, and consecrated by Bishop Roskell of Nottingham. Bishop Roskell, who loved the Hodder Valley, died at Bishops House, on the Brennand road. His grave is opposite the lych-gate.

St. Hubert is the patron saint of hunters – Bowland Forest was once a Royal Hunting Ground. Hubert was a son of the Duke of Aquitaine, mighty in arms, and devoted to the chase. Legend has it that one holy day, Good Friday, as folk were going to church, Hubert set off to hunt, but was checked by the appearance of a stag bearing a luminescent crucifix between its horns. Hubert prostrated himself and from that moment changed his way of life. St. Lambert of Maestricht sent Hubert on a pilgrimage to Rome where the pope, foreseeing Lambert's martyrdom, consecrated Hubert to succeed him.

Whilst in Rome St. Peter appeared to Hubert in a vision and granted him the power to cure people with mental disorders. The name Hubert means 'bright of heart and mind.'

BURHOLME FONT

As Bishop of Maestricht (AD 708) and afterwards of Liege, Hubert was a vigorous missionary through Brabant and the Ardennes.

Hubert and the stag are pictured in the middle stained-glass window at the rear wall of the chapel.

A 20p donation will obtain you a superb little guide to this lovely wayside House of the Lord. (Give it a read and you may find a picture of the racehorse Kettledrum.)

I always reflect awhile before leaving the chapel finding great solace in Hubert's illumination and vision, a cruce salus.

THE RETURN TO DUNSOP

On the way back listen out for the green woodpecker using one of the dead trees in the wood on the left as a sounding board. The mating call is a loud, laughing 'queu–queu–queu-queu.'

Walk down to the road signs at the junction.

Great Spotted Woodpecker

Almost hidden by modern signposting you will find a most ancient stone road distance marker with iron finger-posts. The stone is dated 1739 with initials PM & TG, and informs us: TO HORNBY 10 MS (the old Salter Fell Track/Roman Road,) TO SLADBVRN M : 3, TO CLITHERO 7 : MS, TO LANKSTER 11 : MS.

Turn left and walk on to Dunsop Bridge and a well-earned cuppa at Puddleducks!

Milestone
Dunsop Bridge

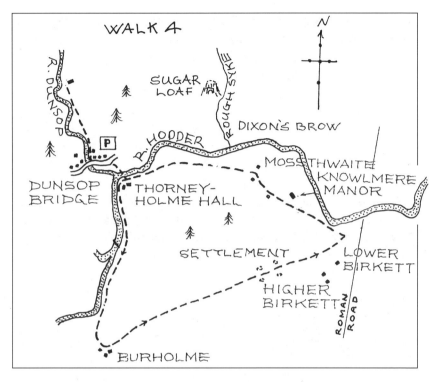

WALK 4

LOST VILLAGE & HAUNTED MANOR

A 4 mile walk with a gentle climb up Fielding Clough to cross the saddle between Hodder Bank Fell and Birkett Fell to gain superb views over both the lower and upper Hodder Valley. We shall have contact with the USA and, maybe, with a troop of phantom riders.

DUNSOP TO BURHOLME

On leaving the car park turn left and walk along the road a short way, to go right, along the avenue of Wellingtonia

to cross the bridge at Thorneyholme. Pass through the gate on the right and follow the Hodder river down, over two fence-stiles to the green, iron footbridge. Follow the path over the rough ground...

Here the Hodder is met by the Langden Brook while the Old Man of Bolland sleeps on with Totridge keeping a 'look out' over the lower Hodder Valley. Notice the old hipping stones that cross the river to Langden Holme.

...to go over stile by old Water Authority iron gate. Cross the field to go over stile by gate and on to go over further stile by gate. Walk up to enter Burholme by stile and footbridge.

Burholme is a working farm, home to Mr. Rodney Spence and family. So we shall respect their living and privacy and not go wandering all over the show in search of all that is to be found here. Enough that we view a few of the 'Quaker' stones set in the barn wall.

Walk past the front of the farmhouse down to the stone-built barn on the left.

BURHOLME

The barn is dated 1619 with the initials of Thomas Swinhulhurst, and below this date some another is inscribed: I JANE LOVE FOR TRU TO W*** AND FAITHFUL I WILL BE (Jane Waln.) Other carved stones on the building bear much faded dates and inscriptions and are known as 'Quaker Stones.'

These stones record Quaker emigration to America from the then village of Burholme and other townships in Bowland during the 17th century.

Nicholas and Jane Waln of Burholme left England with William Penn and sailed for America on the Welcome in 1682 where Penn founded Philadelphia and went on to establish the Quaker colony of Pennsylvania in 1683.

Those early Bowland emigrants to the New World named their new settlement in Pennsylvania after their old village. Burholme, which is today a suburban area of the city of Philadelphia.

Although only a single farmstead today, Burholme was once a village and even had a church. It is recorded in the Domesday Survey of 1086 as 'Bogewrde,' meaning 'the place of the cairn by the bow in the river.'

Some time in the 14th century the village and church were abandoned, the latter being moved to Whitewell when the Radholme deer park was established. The decorated font from Burholme Chapel is now in use as a Holy Water stoop at St. Hubert's Chapel on the Trough Road.

With the decline of the deer park, Burholme re-established itself as a small hamlet. The 1527 Rent Roll records at least six families living here.

Before 1590, dwelling houses were of wood and ling-thatch heather, often comprising only one room. By the mid 17th century wood had given way to stone and only the poorest families still dwelt in primitive cruck-framed houses. However, rebuilding in stone was slow to spread to outbuildings – all barns recorded in Bowland for 1652 were of the timber cruck-framed type.

The farmhouse today at Burholme incorporates two early 17th century buildings and was remodeled in the early 19th century. Notice the huge gable chimney stack.

Archaeological excavations to find the 'lost village' and chapel were undertaken in 1985-6 by my WEA Group under the direction of the late Mr. Chris Spence of Burholme. We located the site of the chapel and recorded the sites of eight buildings and a circular structure thought to be a pinfold.

The higher barn at Burholme is also of great interest. The timbers of the cow stalls come from old dismantled ships brought down from Glasson Dock in the 18th century.

Behind this barn the old village well stands in a small enclosure. Though now dry it was once fed from natural springs.

The farm, and the farmlands at Burholme are exceptionally well managed reflected in the good quality of stock here – cows, sheep, and horses – a credit to the family and a very good example to others.

BURHOLME

BURHOLME TO KNOWLMERE MANOR

Return to cross the foot bridge and stile and walk upstream to go over a fence-stile, and on up the clough to go over next stile. The path takes you up Fielding Clough to go over a ladder-stile onto the moorland saddle.

The Saddle Stone

Fielding Clough makes for a good picnic stop to take in the views below Fair Oak Fell over the lower Hodder Valley.

Walk up the track and on across the moor by way of the marker stones...

This moorland track was once the old road between Whitewell and Newton. It is also an area of Bronze Age settlement. Myself and Jaana found an ancient saddle quern up here among the low remains of hutments and other structures.

...And on down to pass through a wall gate.

Below us is Matril field barn, and before us a magnificent view of the upper Hodder Valley and all the surrounding fells.

Walk down the field to go over fence-stile and on two go over two more stiles down to Knowlmere drive by Giddy Bridge. Turn left along the drive to Knowlmere Manor.

Part of the S.W. Elevation   Knowlmere Manor

KNOWLMERE MANOR

Sited at Grey Gill, the house is built in the Gothic style of the Victorian Era: with its many gables and chimneys it presents an interesting picture and has been used many times as a Television and Film set. The Parkland adjoining the manor is exceptionally well maintained and most pleasing to the eye.

The Manor was built by the Peel family, descendants of Sir Robert Peel, founder of the modern Police Force.

The author and historian Alice Peel resided at Knowlmere in the early 20th century. Her books, 'The Manor of Knowlmere' (Preston, 1913) and ' A Short History of the Parish of Slaidburn,' give one a good picture of former Valley life.

Knowlmere stands upon the site of an ancient village that in turn stood on the site of a Roman cavalry station manned by Sarmation horsemen. The Sarmations were nomadic Steppe warriors brought by the Romans to Britain in around AD 175 to garrison the Brigantian region, their headquarters was at Ribchester, the Roman road from which crosses the Hodder just below Giddy Bridge.

When the Romans left in the early 5th century the many thousands of Sarmations and their families stayed on in east Lancashire and Bowland to breed horses, and founded a vast territorial unit, based  upon Whalley, that was to be known later as Blackburnshire.

Their greatest leader was a man known as 'The Bear,' who came down through legend as King Arthur. His standard was the　dragon and his men were known as dracomen (draconarius,) a title which still lingers in the British army in the form of 'dragoon.' The people of

Wales would later take his standard as their National emblem.

The Sarmation battle standard was a silken wind stock in the shape of a dragon, which hissed wildly when filled with air as its bearer charged into battle, terrifying their opponents.

One of Arthur's greatest battles was fought at Bashall, near Clitheroe. Every year, on the eve of this event, his dracomen rise from the grounds of Knowlmere, mount their horses and with standards screaming charge up the side of Birkett Fell and down through Browsholme to meet their foe at Bassas Brook.

Sarmation Cavalryman with 'dragon' wind-sock standard

Their womenfolk, all shamanesses, wearing their tall conical hats with brims at the base, hover round the grounds of Knowlmere in wild circling motions and are often mistaken for witches. Hodder Valley folk keep to the hearth on such a night.

KNOWLMERE TO DUNSOP

Continue on along the drive to go over stile by gate at Mossthwaite farm.

A good view here of the suspension bridge and Sugar Loaf Knoll.

The track way we are now on is an old coach road, linking the Towneley House of Thorneyholme Hall with the village of Newton.

Follow the track on to go over stile by gate, and on to go over wall-stile on the right by a gateway. Walk down the field on a left diagonal to go over fence-stile in line of trees. Walk on to cross the bridge at Thorneyholme to return to Dunsop.

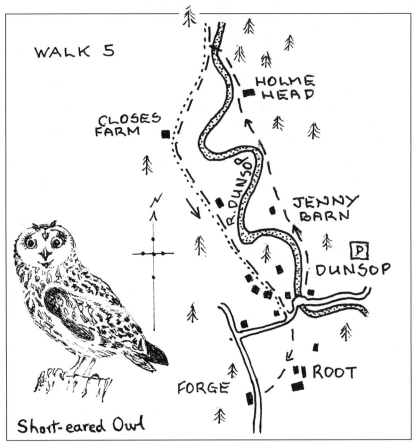

Short-eared Owl

WALK 5

NORWEGIAN WOOD

1¼-mile wander around the village surroundings with a visit to the local blacksmith's forge at Root. A 'Discovery Trail' for all the family.

The Dunsop Valley circular section is great for those who need the assistance of a wheelchair and wish to view the wild valley landscape and wildlife.

DUNSOP VILLAGE POST OFFICE & CAFÉ TO DUNSOP VALLEY

Walk up the lane by the side of 'Puddleducks', passing the new Children's Play Area and then Jenny Barn, to the rear of Holme Head Cottages. Pass through a gate and on to go over the access bridge.

Red Grouse

Before us looms the great mass of Staple Oak fell, home to the red grouse and pheasant – the sporting ground for the well-heeled.

Turn left and walk along the road to the cattle-grid at Closes Farm.

Look back and take in the view. In the distance is the round hump of Middle Knoll, behind which, high on the moors, are the Whitendale Hanging Stones – 'The Centre of the Kingdom'.

To your right, Beatrix Fell rises from the 'Hidden Valley' to meet with Burn Fell. Here was the scene of a tragic accident towards the end of World War Two.

On the afternoon of Tuesday, 2nd January 1945, valley farmers heard the roar of an aircraft's engines in the low cloud above them; it was flying low – too low.

THE LAST FLIGHT OF 42-100322 OF THE 714 BOMBER SQUADRON. 448 BOMBER GROUP, U.S.A.A.F. 02/01/45.

Beatrix Fell ~~ Liberator Crash

Seconds later a USAAF B-24 J Liberator 'Flying Fortress' bomber, its four Pratt & Whitney Twin Wasp engines screaming wildly, emerged from the cloud cover. Horrified, the farmers could only look on as the giant bird smashed into the side of Burn Fell and continued a crazy slide up to the summit where it burst into a towering fireball, machine-gun shells going off in every direction.

Amazingly, most of the crew were thrown or leaped to freedom in the soft bog before the explosion, but four brave airmen lost their lives in the inferno.

13 survivors were brought down the fell by local folk and treated for their injuries at Burn House Farm. Another turned up later having made his own way down the fell to Beatrix Farm.

Today, parts of the aircraft are scattered over the broad ox-ridge of the fell, others are buried deep in the peat haggs.

The three undercarriage legs lie behind the wall at the Trig Point and a large dark patch of earth still remains where the explosion occurred.

I know of six other aircraft crash sites on the Bowland Fells – this was the return flight path to the USAAF Base at Warton, near Blackpool.

Walk down the road to the Forestry Commission Bowland depot.

Long-tailed Field Mouse

What a lovely spot this is – I could happily live here in the timber chalet.

Sitka spruce, of New World origin, was once the most common planted tree in Bowland – a monoculture on which the pine beetle thrived. The new forests hold Scots pine, larch, Norway spruce and Lodgepole pine with an under-story of holly – once a major forest tree. Broadleaved trees are also being re-established.

Walk on to the Crescent.

The timber house you see here came 'flat-pack' from Norway – a gift from the folk of that country for the help they received from Northerners during the last Great War – other houses can be seen in Grindleton.

I have worked on these cedar-built houses and know their construction well. The workmanship and materials are of the finest quality – a far cry from the rubbish named builders throw up today that will not outlive the mortgage repayments – buyer beware.

In the field below the Crescent stands Mill House. I know that it was once a farm but know nothing about an old mill – a good research project for the local school kids.

Walk down to the Memorial Cross.

The cross commemorates the 14 Men of Bowland who gave their lives in the futile war of 1914-1919. The ruling classes have much to still answer for.

"From the troubles of the world
I turn to ducks
Beautiful, comical things…"
By F.W. Harvey 1919.

MILLHOUSE FONT

West Riding
of Yorkshire

Notice the iron WR marker by the kissing-gate opposite – an old West Riding of Yorkshire boundary marker. You will find another on the bridge at Dunsop.

To visit the blacksmith's forge pass through the kissing-gate and walk on to pass through another iron kissing-gate on the right. Walk on to the roadside forge, via gate.

BLACK BOAR FORGE, DUNSOP BRIDGE

As the modern village of Dunsop grew up around a former black-smith's forge this recent Valley enterprise is most appropriate.

The blacksmith, Iain Hogg, whose family were farmers in upper Ribblesdale, grew up not wishing to till land and tend stock but to become a real blacksmith in the true sense of the word.

After an apprenticeship with Ron Carter at Trapp Forge, Simonstone, he went on to establish his own forge in Clitheroe. Iain is now over the moon to have returned to his roots among the folk of the West Riding of Yorkshire.

On a visit to Black Boar Forge you may be fortunate enough to find this 'gentle giant' hammering the red-hot iron forming scrolls, candle-sticks, door brackets, fire-irons and all other manner of ironwork, wrought in the traditional hand-crafted way.

DUNSOP BRIDGE

Iain also specialises in Damascus steel work, being one of the few skilled smiths in this ancient method working in Britain today.

Return through the fields to Dunsop.

The cottage and Working Men's Club by the bridge were once a Dames School run by the Sisters at Thorneyholme.

The village chapel of St. George, known as Root Chapel, stands by the garage petrol station that was once the blacksmith's forge.

The place-name Root (Lower Staple Oak) and Staple or Stump Oak recall a great oak of unusual size, or perhaps a huge stump of bog oak from ancient woodland preserved in the peat moss.

By the river below the bridge is an iron sculpture depicting the Memorial Cross, the Post Office
and the bridge at Dunsop.

As always, the ducks throng around the grassy riverbank waiting to be fed tit-bits from your lunch. These are Mallard ducks. The voice is a deep 'quek ek', and when courting is a high pitched 'weep'. They nest on the ground near the river and are chiefly vegetarian.

mallard rising

ducks landing

"Never look down on a duck –
No creature's quite as clever...
He can waddle and slide
And swim AND dive!
Then fly off for ever and ever."

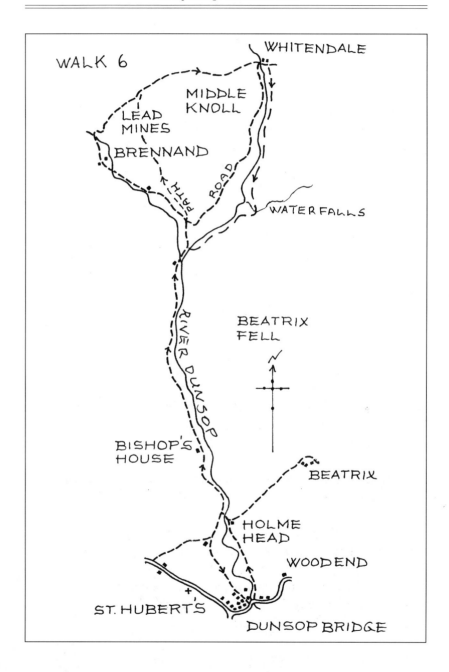

WALK 6

THE BOLLAND SILVER MINES

7½ miles with an easy climb over the saddle of Middle Knoll to take in the Silver Mines at the 'Centre of the Kingdom' and visit the two remotest farmsteads in Lancashire. We return by way of Costy Clough to view the Fairy Glen Waterfalls. Take a bite of lunch and a drink with you and enjoy what will be a most rewarding day.

QUERN STONE DUNSOP B.

DUNSOP BRIDGE TO BRENNAND FARM

Walk along the lane by the side of 'Puddleducks' to the rear of Holme Head Cottages. Pass through the gate and walk on to go over the footbridge. The road takes us up to the valley to the Water Works way beyond Bishops House Cottages.

With very little traffic to look out for, this is a very pleasant river valley wander.

Cross the bridge and walk up to the road junction. The left-hand road takes us to Brennand Farm.

The gateway up on the right opens on to the old miners' track that walkers often use to gain long views over the Brennand Valley en-route for the Middle Knoll saddle.

BRENNAND FARM

BRENNAND FARM

Brennand is yet another former Viking settlement – the name means 'the burning one', some red-haired rover no doubt.

In the days when Bowland was a Royal Hunting Forest the farm was then a hunting lodge and many an old king has rested here after a day's chase. A chapel stood on the site of the barn, a portable altar stone, with five inscribed crosses and the monogram IHS, was found here and is now built into the chapel altar at Whalley Abbey.

BRENAND STONE

Standing by the farmyard is an old mahogany paneled grouse keepers' cabin. During the breeding season the keeper had to spend some time on the fells looking after the birds. At such times, the wheeled cabin would be provisioned and horse-drawn onto the fells, providing the keeper with a mobile living place. During the game season it served as a shooters' refreshment cabin.

West of Brennand, high in the ling below Ughtersik (Millers House), is the deep pool of Brennand Tarn, so deep that the bottom has never been reached. In the depths of these brackish waters is where the monks of Whalley Abbey hid their gold and silver plate from the greedy hands of King Henry VIII. Abbot Paslew went to his death with the secret of how to recover the treasure. Many since have sought in vain, but the tarn holds its secret well.

Below the farm, set into the opposite bank of the river, are the remains of the water-wheel pit for the crusher of the old lead mining enterprise.

BRENNAND TO WHITENDALE

Pass through the farmyard and on down to go over the bridge. Turn right and follow the track up, over stile by gate and on up and around to the left to go over stile by gate.

BRENNAND MINE

We are now in the area of the old mine workings known as 'The Kings Silver Mines in

Bolland', first worked in 1610 by Sir Belvis Bulmer who 'brought the mine to great perfection, and getting great store of Silver Ore'.

Spoil heaps, the low remains of buildings and a reservoir can be seen on the saddle. Scattered about you will find lumps of galena and, occasionally blende. The mines lie off the pathway and are VERY DANGEROUS and should NOT BE ENTERED.

This area, known as 'Good Grave', has been mined for lead and silver since Roman times, and a Romano-British camp is located on the Whitendale side of Middle Knoll.

Follow wall on to go over stile and on over the rough ground, passing the reservoir, down to go through wall-gate. Walk down the steep track to cross the river bridge at Whitendale.

WHITENDALE

'The Dale of the White Heather' – what a lovely setting; a green oasis secluded by the wild high fells. The tall ash tree by the farm and keeper's house is locally referred to as 'the greatest ash in Bowland Forest'.

Pied Wagtail

The short-eared owl is a common sight in the dale, along with pheasant and red grouse.

WHITENDALE TO DUNSOP BRIDGE

Pass through the upper farmyard and follow the wall around to the right to pick up a good track that takes us to the bridge over the waterfalls via gates.

The iron posts marked BCWW that we passed refer to the former Blackburn Corporation Water Works pipeline.

Standing upon the bridge above the tumbling waters, we look up to view the enchanted Fairy Glen.

Tales of elves and fairy folk abound in Bowland lore, like those who dance and sing at Dinkling Green, or those who wash their tiny garments by moonlight at Whitewell.

Here at Costy Clough the tiny folk come to drink and bathe in the twilight just before moonrise, their songs in rhythm with the cascading waters.

One midsummer's eve, the local blacksmith was wandering by this way when he came across a lovely wood nymph bathing by the light of the moon. When she caught his gaze she leaped out of crystal waters and disappeared down a hole in the woodland floor. Upon returning to Dunsop the blacksmith recounted his tale and was surprised to be regaled by the accounts of others' frequent sightings.

Follow the path on and down the zigzags to walk downriver back to the Water Works. Return down the access road to Dunsop Bridge.

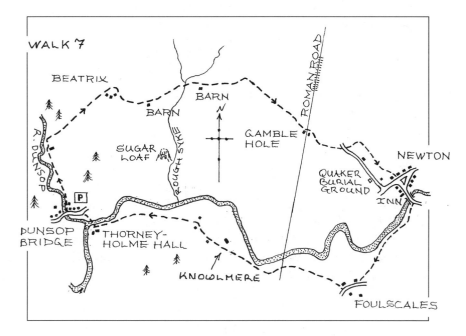

WALK 7

UP HILL & DOWN TO NEWTON

A 6½-mile circular walk with a spot of lunch at the Parkers Arms in Newton village. Lots to see and good tales to tell.

DUNSOP BRIDGE TO GAMBLE HOLE FARM

Follow directions in Walk 2 – 'The Hidden Valley'.

GAMBLE HOLE FARM

Take a 10 pence coin out of your pocket and run your finger-nail along its edge. The serrations you feel were introduced to stop people clipping the edges when coin was made of solid silver and weighing it in return for good coin – a common fraud in former times. The story of that innovation starts right here at Gamble Hole Farm.

lapwings

Robert Parker was born at Gamble Hole Farm in 1731, sixth child and third son of George Parker, yeoman farmer. Robert's father died in 1736, and a year later his mother married John Dixon, a school master. In 1752, the youngest three children – Henry, Robert and Margaret – with their mother and stepfather, moved to Midgely, a tiny hamlet near Halifax. The elder son and two daughters stayed on at Gamble Hole.

Robert later went to study law at Lincolns Inn, London. In 1753 he was admitted an Attorney of the Court of Kings bench. Late in 1753 he returned to Halifax and joined a law partnership. By 1768 he was Chief Lawyer in Halifax and went on to be the major force in the breaking of the infamous Heptonstall Crag Coiners Gang.

The leader of the Crag Coiners was David Hartley, known around the Calder Valley as 'King David'. The two 'hit men' of the gang were Robert Thomas and Matthew Normington, and it was these two in 1769 who tortured and then killed an excise man near Halifax. The poor man's head was roasted over an open fire, slowly till he passed out, and repeated till he died. Tried at York in 1770, they were discharged on the grounds of lack of evidence – people were afraid of the gang and would not speak out against them.

In true Bowland spirit Robert Parker vowed to bring this evil gang to justice. He collected new evidence on the two, but as one could not be tried twice for the same offence, he brought forward a charge against them of highway robbery. Thomas was tried at York on Saturday, 16th July, 1774, and was hanged at Tyburn (now York racecourse) on 6th August of that year. Normington was again arrested in the spring of 1775, and this time was found guilty. He was executed at York and his corpse hung in chains above Halifax next to the bird-eaten remains of Thomas.

David Hartley and one of his henchmen, James Oldfield, were found guilty of their crimes and hanged at York on the 28th April, 1770. Because of the work of Robert Parker and William Deighton, the murdered excise man, the Crag Coiners were broken. The State was moved into action, and coins of a standard weight with milled edges were introduced, so protecting against the debasement of the coinage.

Some foolish people in Calderdale have tried to make the gang into folk heroes, but a more nasty group of Yorkshire thugs you would be hard pressed to find.

You can put the 10 pence back into your pocket now.

GAMBLE HOLE TO NEWTON

From the cattle-grid, take the right-hand track and follow the line of trees to go over a corner wall-stile hidden behind the last tree. Walk down the field to pass through a gate at the far left-hand corner and onto the roadway. Pass over wall-stile opposite and walk on down to cross a little stone bridge over-stream. Walk up to the trees to follow line of old hedge on your right down to go over stile by field barn.

Brown Hares abound here and you may just flush one or two out.

Walk down to pass over stile by gate and on down to go over wall-stile and on into Newton (toilets to the right along the road).

NEWTON IN BOLLAND

I give only a brief description of this lovely village here. I have saved the best for my forthcoming book 'SLAIDBURN, BOWLAND FOREST'.

Newton is home to Mrs. Mary Parker, a true lady of the Forest, who has done more than anyone I know to promote tourism and good management in the Hodder Valley – not to mention all the good work she did (still does) for the Ribble Valley Borough. This year, 2003, she is President of the Hodder Valley Show – well worth a visit.

Standing in the centre of the village is Salisbury Hall. Formerly Newton Old Hall, this was once the home of the Salisbury family who are mentioned as lawyers in Slaidburn in 1729. The red sandstone building to the left of the hall was once the lawyer's office. Notice the two doorways – one was for the lawyer and one for his clerk.

A small roadside shelter houses the old village water-pump.

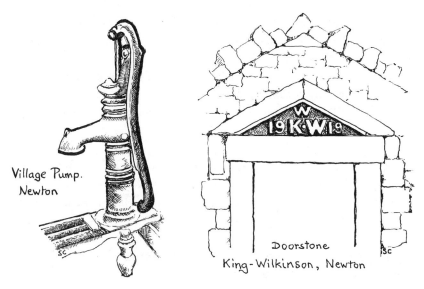

Village Pump.
Newton

Doorstone
King-Wilkinson, Newton

Above the doorway a pediment bears the date 1919 with the initials W.K-W (King-Wilkinson).

The Parkers Arms is a splendid Georgian building displaying a central stepped Venetian window. The inn has a very good restaurant and bar meals are served daily.

Newton Hall, across the way, is a fine Georgian edifice worthy of note, and both buildings present a wonderful frontage to the village when approaching by way of Newton Bridge.

NEWTON TO FOULSCALES

Walk down to Newton Bridge to cross the Hodder.

I remember coming here in the 1960s with a party led by Jessica Lofthouse. She referred to the fields on either side of the road as Goose & Ganders, and pointed out the low remains of an old flax-retting industry. You can still make out the banking of the ponds used for the retting as low ridges running across the fields. I will tell you the full story of textile manufacture in the Hodder Valley in the Slaidburn book.

When walking down the river from here, look out for small burrows driven into the riverbank. These are the nesting holes of sand martins, summer visitors, being light brown above and white beneath with a dark brown stripe across the chest.

Pass through gate on the right and walk directly on and over to the left to go over stile by short wall.

The dry ditch you have just crossed is the old outflow from the flax-retting pits.

Follow river down, over fence-stile and on to cross a small stream at trees. Walk up to the left to pass over a stile by gate and on the same line to go over further stile by gate. Walk on to go over hedge-stile, by the old cottage and barn, onto road.

The keystone above the barn doorway is dated 1870 with an initial 'P'. The cottage has been empty for many, many years. There is a shortage of affordable housing in the Hodder Valley for local people – yet many old farm buildings are falling into decay and ruin. The Valley should not be the province of rich town people alone; local need must be met, otherwise the consequences will be dire.

Notice the old roadside well by the post box.

Walk down to view Foulscales.

FOULSCALES

Here is another former Viking settlement – a place for the breeding of horses. Remember, there was once a Sarmation cavalry station at nearby Knowlmere.

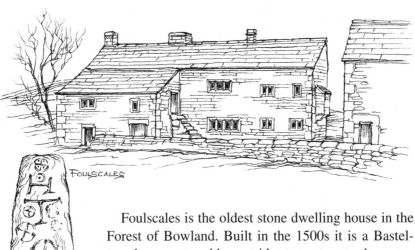

FOULSCALES

Foulscales is the oldest stone dwelling house in the Forest of Bowland. Built in the 1500s it is a Bastel-type house entered by outside stone steps to the upper living floor. Notice the upper low mullioned windows and the medieval latrine (garderobe) set on corbles on the west wall. The ground floor would have once held stock and fodder – providing heating to the upper floor.

The building underwent a change of usage some time during the 17th century – the ground floor being converted for human usage. At that time a branch of the Parker family of Browsholme lived here.

THE FOULSCALES STONE

Also known as the Yolstone/Bonstone, this strange stone once stood behind Foulscales, near Gibbs. The stone displays possible early native chi-rho symbols and some later 16/17th century lettering – H T. given the design and tooling, the stone may have a Celtic 6/7th century provenance – the 'Age of Arthur'.

The Foulscales Stone

For some reason the stone was removed from its site and is now in the hands of the Knowlmere Estate. The stone should be returned to the public domain. The Village Hall at Newton would be the best place to exhibit the stone.

FOULSCALES TO KNOWLMERE MANOR

Walk up the road to enter Knowlmere driveway after passing the two old barns. Walk on…

Notice another suspension-bridge over on your right.

…To go right at the junction down to Giddy Bridge.

The Roman road crosses the Hodder just below Giddy Bridge by the weir. The road is known as Orchinstrett or Orchen Street.

Walk on to view Knowlmere Manor.

KNOWLMERE MANOR

Described in Walk 4.

KNOWLMERE TO THORNEYHOLME

Follow the drive to Mossthwaite to go over stile by gate onto the Old Coaching road. Follow track on, over stile by gate and on to pass over wall-stile on right by gateway. Walk down and on to go over fence-stile in line of trees. Walk on to pass through gates at riverside and on to the bridge at Thorneyholme.

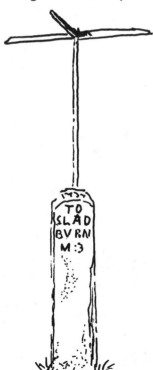

THORNEYHOLME HALL

Built by the Towneley family of Burnley, Thorneyholme was gifted by that family to the Sisters of Notre Dame, a Roman Catholic teaching order, and became a nunnery – the nuns' Dame School was in the houses by the bridge at Dunsop.

The Hall is now an enclave of private dwellings.

TO DUNSOP

Cross the bridge and walk down the avenue of Welingtonia to Dunsop for a well-earned brew at Puddleducks Post Office Café.

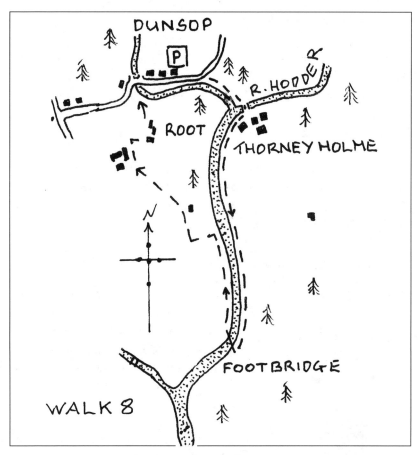

WALK 8

'IN THE MOOD' FOR A RIVERDANCE

1½ miles easy riverbank walking – great views and a little more besides.

On leaving the car park turn left and walk along the road a short way to go right, along the avenue of Wellingtonia to cross the bridge at Thorneyholme. Pass through the gate on the right and follow the river down to the green, iron footbridge, via two stiles.

Before us, resting on his bed of pines, sleeps the Old Man of Bolland. Above him rises Totridge Fell – the site of a Roman 'look-out' station guarding the passage of the Roman road through Bowland.

swift

After crossing the bridge follow the river up to go left at wall and over fence-stile. Walk round the corner and follow the track...

Old Stable near Root

Notice the small square building on your right. This is a stable with two corner wooden mangers. (Watch the rotting roof.) The field here is where Kettledrum, winner of the 1861 Derby, was exercised by the Towneleys.

...to go over stile at gateway. Walk up the banking to go over ladder-stile.

On our left is the Root Centre. Notice the weather-vane on the building above us – horse and jockey, reminding us again of the Derby winner.

Walk on to go over next ladder-stile.

Below us stands Root farm. Jessica Lofthouse, in her book 'Three Rivers' (Robert Hale 1948,) informs us that during World War Two the upper floor of the buttressed barn was the local dance hall – with the grand name of

Corner 8ε.
Manger

Lapwing
(or Pee-wit)

'Root Ball Room.' Here the locals and the soldiers stationed at Dinkling Green and Sykes would dance the night away to the music of Glen Miller and Geraldo on the old phonograph.

Walk down and follow the farm lane to Dunsop Bridge.